The Glory of Sex

How To Live Right in a World Living Wrong

The Glory of Sex

How To Live Right
in a World Living Wrong

by
Edwin Louis Cole

Tulsa, Oklahoma

Unless otherwise indicated, all Scripture quotations are taken from the *King James Version* of the Bible.

Scripture quotations marked AMP are taken from *The Amplified Bible, New Testament*. Copyright © 1958,1987 by the Lockman Foundation, La Habra, California. Used by permission.

Verses marked TLB are taken from *The Living Bible*, copyright © 1971. Used by permission of Tyndale House Publishers, Inc., Wheaton, Illinois, 60189. All rights reserved.

2nd Printing
Over 20,000 in Print

The Glory of Sex
How To Live Right in a World Living Wrong
ISBN 1-56292-079-0
Copyright © 1993 by Edwin Louis Cole
Christian Men's Network
International Headquarters
P.O. Box 610588
Dallas, Texas 75261

Published by Honor Books
P.O. Box 55388
Tulsa, Oklahoma 74153

Dedication

To the new generation of young men and
women who desire to bring back to this
world what a previous generation threw
away. This book is dedicated to them, for
God's glory.

Contents

Acknowledgments

For the Foreword from basketball forward A.C. Green, I extend my deepest thanks. I also want to acknowledge the efforts of my daughter Joann in preparing this manuscript and thank her for all she did. And a big thank you to Keith Provance and all our friends at Honor Books for turning out quality work year after year.

Foreword

by
A. C. Green

In our society sex is a subject that is pretty hard to avoid. This makes it one of the greatest challenges facing young people today. From infancy, a child's perception of sex is shaped by music, videos, magazines, billboards, films, television, peers, and school curriculums, most of which depict sex as something other than God's plan for marriage. Even advertisements are explicit, showing people who would be considered beautiful and cool having sex. The costs of perpetuating these images are staggering in human suffering, death, and expense to society. The sexual revolution of the sixties spawned the broken homes and dysfunctional families of the nineties, which have left an entire generation seeking drugs, gangs, and sexual promiscuity in place of intimacy and love. Many young people today feel rejected and neglected — feelings that continue to breed their hopelessness and despair.

According to research done by the A. C. Green Foundation for Youth with the Center for Disease Control and other agencies, approximately fifty different sexually transmitted diseases are continuing to spread like unrelenting wildfires. One of them, syphilis, has been 100 percent curable for years, yet today it is at an all-time high, raging with greater fury than ever before. One in four Americans between the ages of fifteen and fifty-five will contract a sexually transmitted disease. Two-thirds of those diseases will occur in people under the age of twenty-five. Teenage women are especially susceptible to such diseases. Every day, 15,000 high school students in America are infected with at least one. HPV, which causes cervical and penis cancer, was found in 46 percent of young women who attended the University of California, Berkeley. Every person involved in an extramarital or premarital affair runs a 50 percent risk of catching a disease, not to mention the chances of an unwanted pregnancy, which number over a million each year.

Condoms are not the answer. Condoms cannot possibly stop sexually transmitted diseases that spread from outside contact such as syphilis, herpes, and crabs, to name a few. The HIV virus itself is 450 times smaller than a sperm cell, about one-fifth the size of the holes in latex — the material from which the best condoms are made. Condoms fail up to 36 percent of the time against pregnancies for those depending on them most — you got it — young people.

When people have sex that results in an unplanned pregnancy, pain and regret are always there. A person might have "safe" sex using a condom and escape disease or pregnancy, but there is no condom that keeps someone "safe" from a broken heart or a shattered dream. These are the hazards of extramarital and premarital sex.

Why do I tell you all this? Because as a Christian and a professional basketball player, my passions extend far beyond the courts where I fight to win championships. I desire to influence others, both male and female, to fulfill their potential by pursuing their dreams in accordance with their gifts and talents. Every person who reads this book can become a champion in life. It starts with a decision to not settle for anything less.

The simple solution to the complicated problems surrounding the issue of sex, and the only 100 percent sure way to keep from unwanted pregnancies and sexually transmitted diseases, is abstinence before marriage and fidelity after. That means not getting sexually involved until the time is right — and that means marriage — then staying faithful to marriage for life.

God made sex for enjoyment and procreation. But there are two words connected to God's purposes for every area of our lives — responsibility and timing. Irresponsible sex is the main reason we have so many problems with sexually transmitted diseases and unwanted pregnancies. People do not want to be held responsible for their actions. However, in God's eyes, they are responsible. Responsible sex includes the love and commitment of two people who plan to spend a lifetime together, not just one night. Adding children to the mix is not a decision that is made lightly but is a choice made by two people who have prepared themselves — by waiting until they are married — for one of life's greatest miracles.

People deal with many pressures from society and friends to have sex, and they might think everyone is doing it, but it isn't true. Not everyone is doing it. In my sport, one of the legendary "greats" brags that he had sex with more than 20,000 women. I play basketball with men who take adultery so lightly they joke about the fact that the worst part of an out-of-town game is trying not to smile when they kiss their wives good-bye. Yet I am keeping myself sexually pure and many others just like me are also saying "no" to sex outside of marriage. There are too many risks, and we would miss out on too much in life. Being young and healthy are two of God's most precious gifts. Marriage is another. Yet one poor decision can rob a person of the freedom to live life to its fullest. Acting irresponsibly is not worth ruining the best years of our lives.

The people who are having sex outside of marriage are usually doing it for all the wrong reasons. If someone has sex because others are having sex, where is their individuality? Why give in so easily? If they learned about sex through television, friends, or the occasional pornography that came across their paths, then they don't know the first thing about sex — why God created it and how He intends to bless it. Even married couples need to know these answers. Fact-based, not fear-based, abstinence and fidelity are the point.

In the next few pages, Edwin Louis Cole will spell out the purpose for sex from God's perspective and the reasons God made sex good, pleasurable, and something to be desired. He won't quote any more statistics on pregnancy and disease. He will just explain God's truth from His Word.

Some people will read this book and get angry. Perhaps they will shoot off a letter to tell us "religious" people a thing or two. Others will read it, agree with it, but won't be moved to make a firm commitment and will end up unchanged. Still others will reject it outright, and throw it away.

But many single people will join the growing army of youth who have made a pledge to abstain from sex before marriage. Many will join clubs at church, or receive rings from their parents that signify their purity until they exchange rings on the day of their wedding. Many married people will realize they entered their marriage without the glory of "secondary" virginity, and will renew their marriage vows. Some will understand for the first time what was robbed from them in their youth and will be healed from low self esteem and freed from tormenting doubts and guilt. The people who have this response will forever change their view of life and improve their ability to live to their fullest potential — to become champions.

Even if a person has been sexually active, it is never too late to change. Abstinence has been the right choice for me. If I can do it, so can anyone. Sexual immorality? Not for me. It just isn't worth it.

You take it from here, Ed. Thank you for telling us the truth. We need to hear it.

Introduction

Today sex is treated as an object of humor and virginity is regarded by some as worthless and unwanted. This book stands up to those attitudes and teaches why sex is special to God and virginity is a valuable treasure.

The power of this revelation is hitting the hearts and minds of young men and women. A new generation today is bringing back what a previous generation threw away.

There are many books about sex that deal with the technical, biological, emotional, moral, psychological, and purely pleasurable aspects. But we must learn God's view of sex, according to His Word, in order to really understand what God has given us by providing it. We have to understand why God created sex as He did if we are to enjoy His creation completely.

Everything God created is good — including sex. Man ruins and spoils God's creation by his sinful, selfish nature.

It is important that you read these chapters carefully because if you really understand this message, it will bring you up to a higher level in life. You will have a better understanding of your value as a person and more faith in God as a God Who loves you.

This book is written mostly for teen men and bachelors because God has called me into a ministry to men. But single women also need to understand these principles. Married people, especially, must understand them for the sake of their own relationship as well as to educate their children.

In a day when children are having babies, and young people are having sex at earlier and earlier ages, the special, holy, sacred understanding of sex must be taught and imprinted on our minds. We cannot leave it to a Godless society to try to teach us.

When the Old Testament of the Bible was written, young people were held accountable and treated like adults during their pre-teen years. So I don't treat teenagers like children in this book. I treat them like men and women. Young people are capable of accepting responsibility for their actions from a very early age. Even children recognize truth when they hear it.

Learn the lessons in this book — let them sink into your heart and mind. With prayer, ask God to make them clear to you so you will always remember them. When you finish reading, you should have the answers to your questions about the value of your virginity, the holiness of sex, and the covenant relationship of marriage.

Whether you are a man or woman, single or married, this could well be the most unusual book about sex you will ever read. I trust it will have a lasting impact on you life.

1
Guy Meets Girl

Keith was fourteen years old when he sat in a youth meeting where someone was talking about the value of virginity. He was leaning forward, looking past the brim of his hat at the speaker, but he was only half listening. His mind kept taking fragments of what the speaker said and shooting off in all directions. As his mind raced, suddenly he got a hollow feeling in his chest. Seemingly out of nowhere, yet sparked by the words of the speaker, it dawned on him that he owned something that he could give away only one time. One time! Then it was over. His virginity was a once-in-a-lifetime opportunity, and it was up to him to know when to hang on to it or when to give it away. Whomever he gave it to would receive the only really unique, one-of-a-kind gift he could ever offer in his whole life. Virginity was a one-time only deal. The responsibility of taking care of such a thing felt like a huge weight and a tremendous privilege all at the same time.

Because Keith was a witty, good-looking guy, he already had trouble with his mom for the girls who were always calling his house. He knew he could easily go out and have sex like half his friends already had. But he thought about how cheaply those friends treated their unique gift, and how casually the girls accepted it. He thought about who he could give his valuable virginity to, and decided right then that if it could only happen once — he wanted to give it to "the most beautiful woman in the world," and the only one for him. As his thoughts drifted, he promised himself that he would not have sex until the day he married that special woman.

The meeting continued, but Keith's mind was now gone. He was imagining his wedding day from beginning to end. He saw himself in a white tuxedo, symbolizing the purity he saved for his bride. He pictured how he would watch her walk down the aisle, kiss her after the ceremony, and whisk her away to the most romantic evening imaginable.

The meeting finally ended, the reverie was over but the dream was now alive and for the next two years, Keith held onto that dream. Whenever he thought about it, he might change the order of the wedding or decide on a different honeymoon location. But he was always in white, and she was always beautiful.

Then, during his junior year in high school, it seemed like he met "the most beautiful woman in the world" twice a week. First her name was Laina, then Tricia, then Shana, and the temptations were incredible. But when each Sunday rolled around, he would sit in church and think of being one week closer to his dreams, and he would realize that he was getting stronger every time he said "no."

He graduated from high school with his dream intact, started junior college, and there, on the first day of classes, he met Jennifer, "the most beautiful woman in the world," and in reality the only one for him. After they started dating, he found out Jennifer had kept herself pure, too. In the spring they were engaged. Everything was going along just as he had always dreamed, until they started planning the details of the wedding. When they told her mother that he would be wearing white at the wedding, she blew a fuse.

"I won't have the men in white!" she fumed. "Men always wear dark tuxedos.

White will steal from Jennifer's dress. It's just not proper!"

They tried to explain the reason for Keith wanting to wearing white, but Jennifer's mother insisted that if she was going to pay for the wedding, the pictures would have men in dark tuxedos — and only the bride in white.

After all the temptations that Keith had conquered to achieve his goal, he could not imagine settling for anything less than the dream to which he had clung. He decided he would have to talk to Jennifer's mother privately. That's when a soon-to-be mother-in-law found out what kind of man her daughter was marrying. Although he was still only nineteen, the strength Keith had developed over the years welled up inside him. The self discipline he had practiced for so long kept his words kind but firm. He didn't know where the conversation would end, but he knew he had to talk. Keith started by thanking her for planning such a nice wedding. Then he explained as calmly as he could that he wouldn't let go of his dream. He told her he understood what she wanted and it was fine with him if the other groomsmen wore dark tuxedos. But he would wear white.

Keith's dad mailed me a picture of his wedding along with a letter telling me the preceeding story. The picture was of a wedding party surrounding Jennifer, who wore a beautiful white gown. The groomsmen were lined up in navy blue tuxedos. And standing next to Jennifer was Keith in his tux — totally white from his shoes to his tie. On either end of the wedding party stood proud, beaming parents.

Decisions translate into energy. The decision Keith made in a sacred moment turned into energy that drove him toward his dream. Once he made the choice, he had to continue making the choice daily, but his inner strength increased with every hurdle he vaulted. He was determined, and with the grace of God, his determination held firm.

I receive hundreds of letters from people who have made their lives miserable by having sex before marriage or affairs during their marriage. But today, the tide seems to be turning. Many men and women are making the right decision — like Keith and Jennifer — to keep themselves sexually pure until the day of their wedding and then remain loyal to their spouses after. The promiscuous "sexual revolution" of the sixties is giving way to a new sexual revolution led by a new generation who stand for moral purity. They are bringing old-time morals into a new, high-tech age.

Every individual is created to be unique — similar to, but not just like any other person in history. As a result, every person will respond to events and information in different ways. But we all share common human traits. We all have emotions, thoughts and the power of our own will. Beyond that, we also share in the traits of our sex — whether male or female. New brain research confirms what most people know by common sense: males and females are different. Not only are our bodies different, but our brains are different, too.

Keith experienced dreams and temptations that are especially common to men because men are strongly motivated by sight. Men want so badly to have a beautiful woman that the temptation is sometimes almost overwhelming. Women, on the other hand, have more on their minds. As a result, they generally talk more than men, and they are usually motivated more by words than by sight. It doesn't take a guy a long time to learn how to get to first base with a woman. "I want your body," doesn't usually work! He may be thinking, "I want your body," but he says, "I love you." Those are the three most powerful words in human language. Those three words can topple governments, launch ships, and send dignified people into handsprings across a park.

Women can become deceived by a sweet-talking man even when his actions don't measure up to his words. In the same way, men can become deceived by a beautiful woman, even when they know that she is lying to them. These are very common traps that people get caught in — the temptations have to be determined so we won't fall for them.

Men and women were created to bring different purposes and roles to life, especially into a marriage relationship. The differences cause the two to complement each other, which brings balance and blessing to a family.

In the beginning of human history, God created man "in his image"[1] and for His glory. The Bible says that Adam was alone. Being alone can be a blessing, but being lonely never is. When Adam's alone-ness degenerated into loneliness, it was a curse rather than a blessing.

Living in the Garden of Eden, Adam enjoyed friendship with God, but he wasn't a peer to God because God has no peers. For love to be love, there must be an object to love. Adam found himself without anyone to love. In God's wisdom, he caused Adam to fall into a deep sleep, removed a rib from him and formed a perfect counterpart for him. Adam called her Eve.

God did not create Eve from the dust of the earth because He had already put His characteristics and "image" into Adam. If God had made a new creation from anything other than what was already in Adam, He would have created an inferior being. Instead, He took a part of Adam and created a living being that was similar to, and equal to Adam.

The rib God used to make the woman was symbolic of certain qualities He took away from Adam to put into Eve. The qualities that God placed in the woman are those things we now consider to be the woman's feminine nature. God has in His nature all the characteristics we see in both men and women. God is perfectly balanced in being a watcher and listener, a nurturer and provider, the masculine and feminine.

When a man and woman marry, God says that in their marriage the two become one. They are united as "one flesh."[2] This represents bringing back together the Godly characteristics that were first placed in Adam, then separated into male and female.

Woman was created from man. Ever since, man has come from woman in pro-creation. God's balance and perfection are evident.

With such a perfect creation, where do people go so wrong? What ever happened to the "one flesh" part of marriage? Why don't people just stay married instead of getting divorced? And, with all the temptations people face, how do the Keiths and Jennifers of this world stick to their decisions? We can answer these and other questions by straightening out the distorted information people receive.

2

The Sign
of the Covenant

Sex education is a "hot issue" these days because it is a hot topic among people who have heated passions. One side is passionately concerned about the moral issues and the role models who teach about sex, and the other is passionately engaged in it. Who teaches young men and women?

In a recently published newspaper poll of 1000 teenagers, split roughly in half between males and females, 38 percent were found to learn about sex "on their own," 23 percent from friends, 20 percent at home, and 12 percent at school.

Only one boy in seven learns about sex at home, and there are not enough who learn about it at church to show up in the research data. And, only 2 percent of those interviewed said they thought sex should be taught in school. The church is rarely identified as the place to learn the truth about sex. Thank God this is now changing. The Scripture says, "The priest's lips should keep knowledge, and they (the people) should seek the law at his mouth: for he is the messenger of the Lord of hosts." The church is the place to learn!

These same interviewees thought that a girl could not get pregnant the first time she had sex, that condoms ruin sexual pleasure, that oral copulation is not sex and that masturbation is good. Fifty percent admitted they had already engaged in sex while still in high school.

The poll also estimated that an average of 9,230 suggestive comments or scenes representing sexual intercourse are shown on American television each year.

Television executives have stated that television does not influence people, yet they charge as much as $900,000 for a 30-second advertisement because of the influence it has. A study showed that young people who were exposed to large doses of programming with sexually immoral activity were affected in their basic values. Their tolerance for crime rose and their sympathy for victims dropped.

According to the Bible, sex is more than a pleasurable act or erotic experience. Sex is the sign of the covenant of marriage. Sex is a divinely ordained, holy sign of a blood covenant. In other words, when a man and a woman make a commitment to one another before God, and they declare their desire to become "one flesh," then God provides an actual blood covenant to seal their commitment. This blood covenant is established when the marriage is consummated, which means the first time they share sexual intercourse together.

A blood covenant is the highest covenant that can be made between two people. God made His covenant of salvation through the blood Christ shed on the cross of Calvary.

God is a God of covenants. When God told Abraham that He would make him a father of many nations, at first Abraham laughed because he was already ninety-nine years old, and his wife Sarah was past the age of having children. But the Bible says that "Abraham believed God"[1] and that he and God entered into a covenant relationship. Abraham decided to believe God, and God promised to bring about what He had said.

As a physical sign of the agreement they made, God changed Abram's name to Abraham, which means "a father of many nations,"[2] then commanded him and all the men in his household to be circumcised as a sign of their covenant.

Circumcision, the cutting off and casting away of the male foreskin, was symbolic of what occurs when God cleanses the heart of a man. (By God's Spirit, He cuts off our sin when we ask for forgiveness.) The foreskin represented uncleanness, and the casting away of the foreskin represented the putting away of uncleanness in a man's life. The physical represented what happened in the spirit.

Circumcision was a matter of the heart first and of the flesh second. If cleansing the heart did not come first, then the physical act would have no meaning. Circumcision, because flesh is cut, causes blood to be shed. The Bible says, ". . . without the shedding of blood, there is no forgiveness of sins."[3]

Within the next year, Abraham saw God's promise come to pass, and Sarah had a baby boy whom they named Isaac. Eventually, Abraham had so many descendants that they formed a nation known as

Israel, and Abraham became as God had said, "a father of many nations."

This may make some nervous, but don't worry — we don't have to cut ourselves anymore. The New Testament version of the covenant of circumcision is baptism. Baptism, like the covenant of circumcision and marriage, involves an internal act of faith and an external expression of that faith. When Jesus came and shed His blood on the cross to make a new covenant with humanity, He made the way for man to be "circumcised" in his heart through belief in Him. Man's heart could now be purified of uncleanness through Christ.

Baptism is an act of identification with Jesus Christ — His life, death, burial, resurrection and ascension. It reveals openly before the world what has happened spiritually and internally.

In *The Living Bible* version of Colossians 2:11,12, Paul says, "When you came to Christ he set you free from your evil desires, not by a bodily operation of circumcision but by a spiritual operation, the baptism of your souls. For in baptism you see how your old, evil nature died with him and was buried with him; and then you came up out of death with him into a new life because you trusted the Word of the mighty God who raised Christ from the dead."

Water baptism is the believer's testimony that he has repented of his sinful life, has been crucified with Christ (has died to sin), has been buried with Him (the old nature is dead) and has been raised with Him to live eternally. The symbolism of baptism is only meaningful if the heart and soul have first experienced salvation. It is meaningless otherwise.

What does all of this have to do with sex? Circumcision and water baptism are both external signs of an internal work in a relationship. Circumcision was, and water baptism is, an external evidence of an internal work. Likewise, sex between a man and a woman is the external evidence of the covenant they have already entered into with each other in their hearts.

The following columns show this a little more clearly. Notice that the results of each covenant bring glory to God. We were ultimately created to glorify God in the first place.

HOLY COVENANT	INTERNAL WORK	EXTERNAL WORK
Abraham	Circumcised heart through faith in God	Circumcised flesh

Result: Righteousness from entering a blood covenant, bringing glory to God.

HOLY COVENANT	INTERNAL WORK	EXTERNAL WORK
Jesus	Acceptance of redemption through shed blood	Water baptism

Result: Righteousness from entering a blood covenant, bringing glory to God.

HOLY COVENANT	INTERNAL WORK	EXTERNAL WORK
Marriage	Commitment, unity, love	Sex

Result: Righteousness from entering a blood covenant, bringing glory to God.

Marriage establishes a covenant relationship, sealed by the sexual union. This is why God wants both the man and woman to be virgins when they marry. The marriage covenant, like other covenants God has established, begins in the heart. The love between a man and a woman calls for commitment. Living together is involvement. Getting married is commitment. The love and commitment they have for each other begins the process of "becoming one." This means the two become a unity of one in spirit through marriage. On the day of their wedding, they recite vows, confess love, and "plight their troth" before God and a gathering of witnesses. This vow is the confession of their faith.

When a man and a woman get married as virgins and have their first intimate sexual experience, her hymen is broken. This causes the shedding of blood which flows over the man's part during their intercourse. To God, this is the physical evidence that the couple has entered into a covenant relationship together through the shedding of blood. It is the external evidence of an internal work.

The blood covenant entered into by a husband and wife is symbolic of the covenant God established with His people through the shedding of Christ's blood. Marriage is sacred. It is meant to be a blood covenant.

Through virginity a man and a woman can experience the special holiness of a covenant relationship. Virginity is meant to be a glory — to self, spouse, and especially to God. Virginity is the greatest, most unique, loving and holy gift a person will ever give in a human relationship. People have it free at birth, but guarding and keeping it costs.

Don't let some cheap, momentary relationship in the back of a van, at a cheap motel, on a sandy beach blanket or in the hushed whispers of the living room rob you of the greatest moment of your life!

Instead, do what the Bible says and "Present your bodies a living sacrifice, holy, acceptable unto God, which is your reasonable service."[4] Once you have presented your body to God as a living sacrifice, hold it in that "glory" so you will be able to present it to your wife or husband in the same way on your wedding night. If you are thinking, "Too late for me!" keep reading.

3

Sex Before Marriage

For years young men and women have been playing out a scenario like this:

Guy meets girl. Guy dates girl then tells her, "I love you." Time passes and eventually he says, "I love you so much I can't live without you. Let's have sex." She agrees. They have sex. She gets pregnant. She goes to him with her pregnancy and says, "I'm pregnant. Let's get married." But he says, "Not me, Baby" and walks away.

The truth is, he never did love her. He merely "lusted her." All he wanted was to benefit himself at her expense, and that is lust. Lust is a counterfeit of the love that God created. Love desires to benefit *others* at the expense of *self*. Lust desires to benefit *self* at the expense of *others*. If he had really loved her in the way God loves, then he would have considered her more than himself.

This is an important step to understanding God's view of sex, because God made sex for loving and giving, not for lusting and getting. Yes, God created sex. The devil did not create it. Satan is not a creator. He is a counterfeiter. God made sex good. Man, under Satan's influence, makes it bad.

God creates the positive, builds on a positive, and always ends on a positive. The ways of love are positive. Lust is a negative.

The consequence of going the way of the world, the way of lust, is broken trust, perhaps an unwanted pregnancy, and maybe some disease. The benefit of following God's way, the way of love, is that it will bring blessing, peace, joy, into the one's life, and honor to God.

Too often, when pregnancy is the result of lust, abortion seems to be the answer. Some think, "If we just get rid of the baby, we'll get rid of the problem." Wrong! Abortion won't solve the problem. Abortion is simply an atonement for sin, a blood sacrifice to the god of convenience. Abortion can cause physical damage as well as emotional and psychological damage that may never heal. If it does heal, it may take years. Abortion can be painful — more painful than having the child would ever have been. Seek counsel from your pastor and others before making that decision. It is better to obey God's Word in the first place when tempted: "Flee fornication."

God made a rule for Israel in the Old Testament. If a man *took* a woman's virginity, he had to take care of her for life. If a woman *gave* up her virginity outside of marriage, she was to be killed.

Does that leave any question that God expects both the man and the woman to be virgins at the time of their marriage? Because of the small amount of blood that is shed when the hymen is broken, it is possible to prove the virginity of a woman. If someone proved that a woman had lost her virginity before marriage, her husband could have the marriage annulled. She would not be his responsibility. If the woman had not been raped or lost her virginity through forcible sexual assault, they assumed she had voluntarily submitted to sexual intercourse before marriage, against God's commandment.

In case there was a dispute, God gave explicit instructions on how to settle the matter. The evidence of the woman's purity was to be found in her "tokens of virginity," which meant blood on the sheets. The parents of the bride were to give the newlyweds a set of "bedclothes" for the couple's first night of marriage and their initial act of sexual intercourse. After their first night together, if the man charged that his new bride was not a virgin, then the bride's parents were to bring the sheets used that night and spread them before the elders of the city as evidence concerning their daughter's virginity.[1]

If the tokens of virginity were found, it was evidence that the man had lied in an attempt to get out of the marriage and defraud his new bride and her parents. His charge, if false, was considered slander against a "virgin of Israel" and incurred a severe penalty. First, the husband was to pay the parents of the bride a fine for bringing a false charge against their daughter. Second, he was to continue the marriage without any further opportunity for divorce.[2]

This meant that he could not put her out and make her fend for herself, hoping to find someone who would marry her as a divorced woman. The man's penalty was the responsibility to provide and care for a woman he obviously didn't love.

But, if his charge was true — if the woman was not a virgin, though representing herself to be — then the husband was given the annulment he desired. Her penalty for defrauding her parents and husband was to be brought before the people of the city and be stoned to death. She had "wrought folly in Israel by playing the whore in her father's house."[3] The penalty for losing her virginity was death.

Why was the punishment so severe? The punishment was severe enough that the "fear of the Lord"[4] would come upon all of Israel so they would get rid of evil, including sexual immorality. God knew, of course, the tragic results of sin and wanted to save them from the hurt and pain that would follow. But then, there are always those who don't really believe that God loves them and is working *for* them, not *against* them.

Just think what would happen in our country today if this same law was in effect. We would have a financial crisis, for one thing! Our courtrooms and doctors' offices would be full of people arguing about the "tokens of virginity." We'd probably have a lot less sexually transmitted diseases and abortion. For sure, more people would think twice about losing their virginity.

Before continuing, let me point out something to young men. Men are responsible for what they say about women. Men receive a penalty or curse for lying about a woman. A man who, after a date, brags about his "conquest," when in reality there was none, slanders a woman and causes her the loss of her reputation. Men who do this are subject to the judgment of God.

I warn you against making any statement of untruth regarding a woman's virtue. In fact, if you are guilty of having done it, ask God to forgive you for your sin of slander. You have brought a false charge against God's handmaiden, and it will not go unpunished.

When I mentioned this to a group of college men, their leader told me it answered his question as to why there seemed to be such a curse on campus, especially in some men's "frat houses." Men cannot violate God's commandments, or His children, and not expect His judgment.

Unfortunately, in many church youth groups today, young people go to church regularly but in their private lives don't have the fear of the Lord and don't have self discipline over their desires to do evil. The first Christians understood they had to walk in the "fear of the Lord" and the "comfort of the Holy Ghost." If a young person only walks in the comfort of the Holy Ghost and does not fear the Lord, then he or she doesn't see any reason not to do evil. Without that restraint, lasciviousness becomes the rule, which means "loosed-from-restraint living." In Melbourne, Australia, as I left the building after a men's meeting, a young man stopped me to challenge my teaching.

"Do you mean to tell me that as a single man I'm supposed to live without sex?" He asked boldly obviously wanting to challenge me.

"Do you believe the Bible?" I asked calmly.

"I do," he said.

"The Bible says that fornication is a sin, and that outside of marriage sex is not to be indulged in," I said.

He countered me saying, "That was meant for centuries ago when the standards of behavior were different."

"Don't you believe in personal salvation?" I asked.

"Yes, but the way to live it has changed," was his excuse.

"Sir," I said, "the Bible and its standards have never changed. You obviously want to believe only the portions of Scripture that suit you, but you are not interested in truly living your life for God." He was shocked that I didn't back down and walked away with his head down. People like that are the ones Jesus rebuked when He said they could justify their every inconsistency. They can find an excuse for believing one thing one day and another the next.

God never gave His Word so that we could take portions of it and justify our lifestyle. That is what cults do. God requires us to take our lives and make them conform to His Word. We submit to the image and will of God; we don't make God into *our* image according to *our* will. God's Word is the source of our faith and the rule of our conduct. We can believe God and make the most of our salvation or try to believe only enough to get saved from hell and end up in misery.

God has no double standards — man does, God doesn't. God expects both men and women to be virgins when they marry. It is my belief that the divorce rate in America is in direct proportion to the rate of people who lose their virginity before marriage.

I sat in my office one day with a married couple who were in constant turmoil. Regardless of how much they talked things out and how many hours of counseling they received, their marriage remained an absolute mess.

Finally, in a counseling session that turned out to be our last, I asked the two of them, "Did you have sex together before you got married?" Rather sheepishly, they admitted that they had. Then the wife began to cry and weep. Her husband and I sat there absolutely amazed at how much emotion welled up in her over this one incident that had taken place years before.

As she cried, I turned to her husband and asked him, "Have you ever asked her to forgive you for causing her to lose her virginity before you were married?"

He said he had not.

"This would be a good time to do it," I said.

That couple never had to come to see me again. The healing process began and peace started to reign in their lives and in their home. If only this couple had lived by God's Word before they married, they could have avoided years of pain and marital conflict. But when they realized that they had not only violated God's plan for them but also that they had violated each other, they were able to own up to what they had done and began to be joined together as "one flesh."

Recently a young man told me about a problem he was having with his girlfriend, but his account just didn't sit right with me. "It sounds to me like you aren't telling me everything. Did you have sex with this young lady?" I asked. He insisted that he hadn't.

As he continued to give me sketchy details, I became edgy with him because he was giving me symptoms of a problem between them that I recognized as usually involving sex. Finally I pinned him down and said, "I want to ask you a question, and I want you to look at me when you answer. Did you have sex with her?"

"She's still a virgin," he replied.

"That tells me nothing," I said. "Did you have sex with her?"

"Yes, we had oral sex, but she's still a virgin."

There he stood, too ashamed to tell me the truth, knowing in his heart that it was wrong, but trying to insist in word and deed that it wasn't sex!

Remember, sex was made for loving and giving, not for lusting and getting. This young man was "lusting" his girlfriend, not loving her. All he was thinking about was his personal pleasure at her expense. No wonder he had a problem. She probably felt like some commodity he used that had no value as a person.

Men are to love their wives as God loves them, the way that Christ loved the Church. People who date can prepare for marriage by putting others first. If you can't date without lusting, stick with a group.[5]

The way you live as an individual has an effect on this world. By your relationship to God, you directly influence what happens all around you. Every man who renounces sin grows in strength and authority and makes an impact on the world around him.

The world stands up and takes notice of the man who walks in the fear of the Lord.

It is up to those in the Church to bring a measure of the fear of the Lord into their nation. To the degree that the nation loses its fear of the Lord, it will lose its influence in the world. But the nation that fears the Lord will make an impact on the world.

4

Pornography,
Masturbation and Lust

You may have made a decision not to engage in fornication or adultery, but you may still be fighting an ongoing battle with lust because everywhere you turn you see sex and are continually tempted to entertain impure thoughts. You may be thinking that those thoughts are rising up from within you, but, in reality, you may be being influenced by the spirit of others.

Say, for example, that you feel pure in your spirit when you pray in the morning, but you feel spiritually disturbed or depleted after arriving at school or work. You may need to take a serious look at your environment because something in it could be affecting your spiritual state. The problem may be as simple as a billboard you pass each day or your choice of radio station when you're getting ready. Even though that billboard or dee-jay may not be blatant enough to attract your conscious attention, subliminally they may be suggestive or provocative enough to affect your spirit without you even realizing it. The communication of the spirit of that dee-jay or billboard, and the men and women behind them, may create a serious problem for you. It may not come from your own spirit, but from theirs. Nevertheless, you need to realize you are affected by it, then do something about it.

Because seducing spirits are so real, ask God to help you become aware of the spiritual influences which surround you in your daily life and routine.

Although we may not even be aware of some of the spiritual influences that are affecting us, there are other spiritual influences of which we are quite aware. Pornography is one of them.

Pornography, whether in a magazine or on the screen, is specifically designed to help you entertain lustful thoughts. The more you entertain those thoughts the less control you have over them and before you know it, they have created a place for themselves in your mind.

Not only does pornography encourage its readers to create an image in their mind, but it also entices them to fantasize about it. Usually these fantasies involve an erotic act that only can be satisfied with someone else or by masturbation.

Once an image is created in the mind, that picture actually becomes an idol. The habit of masturbation becomes an act of worshipping that idol. Eventually, it creates a stronghold in the mind and becomes a trap.

Whether single or married, getting into a habit of masturbation can affect a person in a harmful way. No matter what any psychologist says or how any popular author attempts to justify or explain away the guilt, there is a consequence — perhaps not physiologically, as some old wives' tales say, but at least psychologically. All sin promises to please and serve but only desires to enslave and dominate. Masturbation promises to please your lusts and serve your desires without consequences, but it only desires to enslave and dominate you eventually.

Some people think I'm old-fashioned for preaching this, but I encounter men all the time who have lost all sense of balance because of habitual masturbation. One man asked, "How many times a day would you consider habitual?" That is reason enough to teach it!

When people tell me about someone whose behavior is inconsistent and radically altered, one of the first questions I ask is, "Is it a woman or pornography?" Inevitably, the change in behavior is related to one or the other. Because pornography pollutes, contaminates and infects both the mind and spirit, the result is confusion. It brings inconsistency of life, a mental fog, spiritual weakness and separation from friendship with God.

Jim desired to be someone whom others would look up to and hoped someday to become an evangelist. But he reminded me of what my friend Jack Mackey once said: "Illusions of grandeur are not visions of greatness." Fact and fantasy are not compatible.

He saw himself as a popular young man with a strong desire to accomplish great things for God, but others saw him as an inconsistent young man who changed from day to day. He was a constant problem to the ministry and minister alike because he wasn't teachable.

Oh, he *heard* the Word, but he didn't *do* the Word. He was a make-believer, not a believer. Jim couldn't overcome his own lusts. Periodic bouts with porno films, magazines and cable movies caused mental dullness that resulted in his inconsistencies. Sin always changes behavior. It has ever since the Garden of Eden when it began with Adam.

What Jim and many of the young men and women that participate in pornography are looking for is intimacy. But pornography doesn't produce intimacy. Instead of closeness, it produces distance. Pornographers often end up impotent, unable to have sex. Pornography, like sin, promises to please and serve but only desires to enslave and dominate. One young lady and her husband experienced first-hand the devastating toll that pornography takes.

At the close of a noon prayer meeting I had conducted for the employees of a large East Coast ministry, a young woman drew me to one side for private prayer.

"I have a problem," she said, a little shyly.

"What is your problem?" I asked.

Her face drew tight and tears welled up in her eyes. "I don't really know," she stammered, biting her lip, "but my husband says I have a problem."

I tried again. "What does your husband say your problem is?"

"He says I don't understand him," she finally said, agonizing over each word.

"What don't you understand?" I asked.

Suddenly, the young lady began to weep, bitterly, from deep within.

"My husband keeps magazines by his side of the bed," she gasped quietly between sobs, "*Playboy*, *Penthouse* and those others. He says he needs to look at them before he can have sex with me. He says he needs them to stimulate him."

She squeezed out the sentence, tears flowing down her face.

"I told him he doesn't really need those magazines, but he says I don't understand him. He says if I really loved him, then I would understand why he has to have the magazines, and I would let him get more of them."

"What does your husband do for a living?" I inquired.

"He's a youth minister."

I stood there, shocked, as I realized what she was telling me. Her husband was a youth minister who kept a pile of pornographic literature by his bed!

"Your husband may be a youth minister," I responded evenly, "but he is also a pornographer."

The woman's head snapped to attention. It was as if I had slapped her solidly across the face. She had never expected to hear her husband described as a pornographer. And yet, his lifestyle made him exactly that.

The pornography that her husband looked at to bring intimacy only brought distance and impotence into his marriage. What many people don't realize is that pornography is actually a counterfeit for prayer. Pornography promises to produce what prayer alone can produce — intimacy.

We become intimate with the One to Whom we pray, for whom we pray and with whom we pray. So, the greatest intimacy a man and woman will ever know in their relationship will come out of times of prayer together. Nothing else will produce the intimacy and interpersonal relationships that prayer will. Consider the following comparisons:

KINGDOM OF GOD POSITIVE	KINGDOM OF SATAN NEGATIVE
Jesus is Lord	Self is Lord
Love	Hate — emotionally
	Lust — morally
Sex	Perversion
	Fornication
	Adultery
Prayer	Pornography
Intimacy	Distance
	Impotence
Blessing	Guilt

In creation, God created the entire earth in the positive. Man, through sin, recreated it in the negative. God creates, but Satan counterfeits. When it comes to love, there is freedom but lust gives a heavy burden. Love is satisfying, but lust is insatiable.

God's power is released in your life to the degree that you are obedient to Him, and no more. So if you disobey Him by constantly following your lusts, you won't have His power. All God's promises are conditional. His love is not conditional, but His promises are. To get His promises, we have to meet His conditions. To live on the left side of the chart, in the Kingdom of God, we have to refuse what is on the right side of the chart, in the kingdom of Satan.

"To him that knoweth to do good, and doeth it not, to him it is sin."[1] When you do your part, God will do His part. He gives you His Holy Spirit to keep you pure in thought, word and deed. Instead of allowing lustful thoughts to continue to dominate your mind, program your conscience mind with the Word of God, and don't let the perversion of the world affect you.

Renew your mind daily. Read God's Word, and apply it to your life. You're never too young to start.

5

Freedom From the Effects of Abuse

I was in my hotel room when the phone rang. It was the grandmother of the eight-year-old girl with which I had prayed with at a church the night before.

During the course of the meeting that night, I had prayed for women who had been abused. One out of every four women has been abused or sexually assaulted by some man during her girlhood, and that ratio is rising. Men and women, boys and girls who have been abused and misused need healing from the emotional hurt. For most of them, counseling is not even considered. The majority of these victims simply stuff the experience into the back of their minds hoping never to remember it again. But it becomes a stumbling block in relationships and ruins their ability to experience genuine love.

That night, at the prayer for female victims, the grandmother stood with her granddaughter and the other ladies. I did what I normally do at that time and stood before those women in the place of the man, or men, who had hurt, abused, violated or misused them. I asked them to forgive me in his place. It is always a moving moment.

After asking them to forgive, it is common for me to pray with them, leading them in a prayer of release. This prayer is simple but powerful as the Spirit of God works in the hearts, minds and spirits of those who pray it.

The grandmother told me on the phone what happened after the meeting when she took her granddaughter home. The precious little eight-year-old had been raped when she was six. It left her so hurt that she couldn't stand to stay with babysitters, so her grandmother kept her when her mother worked.

"I took my granddaughter home last night and put her to bed," the grandmother reported. "After I tucked her in, before I prayed for her, I asked her what Jesus had done for her that night.

"She looked at me and said, 'Grandma, Jesus made me feel just like I did before it ever happened'."

God can do more in one touch of His Spirit than the whole world can do in all of our lifetimes put together. For some people, it takes longer to let it all out because of the wall of bitterness, guilt, resentment and even hatred that has built up over the years. For others, the years just add momentum once they decide to forgive, and it all comes pouring out in a flood as the Spirit of God unlocks what has been held back for so long.

This little girl is only one of thousands of people who have suffered the consequences of a man's sin. Consider this letter:

"Dear Dr. Cole:

"I hate men. My first and real father was an alcoholic. He physically abused my mother, sister, and me. My stepfather has physically abused me and my sister since we were eleven years old. To this day, I won't stay in the same room with him — it still happens.

"No, my mother doesn't know. I'm afraid to tell her because she won't believe me. My sister even said if I told Mom, she would deny it.

"My dad claims to be a Christian. It makes me want to vomit when I sit in the choir loft at church and have to look at him sitting there in the church singing. He makes me sick. *I hate him!* I have tried to forgive him, and when I went and told him I had forgiven him, he just laughed at me and acted as if he hadn't done anything wrong.

"He's a member of the church. I have talked to the pastor about this; he says he doesn't feel he should approach him at this time. Why? Doesn't anyone care about me — my feelings?"

Jesus does.

Such cases are the very reason the Lord has called men like me to minister to people so they can be free from what others have done to them. This is what I call "the principle of *release.*"

The principle of *release* is one of the most powerful principles Jesus ever gave us. It comes from John 20:22,23 where Jesus is talking with his disciples. *The Amplified Bible* version of this passage is the clearest:

"And having said this, He breathed on [them] and said to them, Receive (admit) the Holy Spirit!

"[Now, having received the Holy Spirit and being led and directed by Him] if you forgive the sins of any one they are forgiven; if you retain the sins of any one, they are retained."[1]

In other words, if you forgive anyone his sins, they are forgiven (released), and if you do not forgive, they are not forgiven. You keep what you do not release.

Notice though, that Jesus said, "Receive ye the Holy Ghost" before He gave the principle of release. To forgive as God forgives, it must be done in the power of His Spirit. We cannot do it as an exercise of human faith. Jesus knew what we needed, and He prayed to the Father to send His own Spirit into our hearts so we would have His power, grace and truth to live our lives for Him.

In a recent meeting where I taught this, a woman came to me with a joyful face. "I had a hard time figuring out why I never felt good enough to be a wife or mother — until I heard about the principle of release. My virginity was taken from me when I was five, and I just realized that was the reason I could never feel deserving. I always felt like I was less than a real woman. Tonight I forgave the ma who did it, and for the first time in my life I consider myself to be a real woman."

Negative sexual experiences like these don't just fade away. Unless they are dealt with, they sink deep within a person and cause all kinds of problems. Any pastor, psychologist or social worker who has done any amount of personal counseling will tell you that. People sometimes go through life with the memory of that nagging, unfinished business deep inside their spirit. That's why they never fully experience the joy of the Lord in their sex life.

Another woman, whom I heard about from a pastor, was only sixteen years old when she was gang raped by six men in a van. They were ready to kill her when a police car was spotted driving by; instead, they threw her out of the van and sped away.

Now, years later, she was a beautiful wife and the mother of three children. Inside though, she still ached from the pain caused by those ungodly, perverse attackers. She still battled the feelings of shame, hate, guilt and uncleanness that came when her virginity was so violently stolen from her.

After hearing the principle and praying the prayer of release, she called her pastor to give him the wonderful news that she was finally healed of that nightmare. The Holy Spirit had renewed her mind, spirit and body. She told her pastor that for the first time in her life she desired her husband sexually. She was free — free to love.

It's not just women who have suffered, but men have suffered as well. In San Antonio, after I had prayed with abused women, a man spoke up loudly before the entire audience, "What about us men?" It startled everyone, and I honestly replied, "I'm sorry. It just never occurred to me to include the men. If you need help, let me pray with you now."

He was a schoolteacher. He had been molested as a boy by his own father and brother. Because of it, he battled a spirit of homosexuality. He desired a normal heterosexual life, but thought it never would, or could be for him. When he forgave and prayed the prayer of release, he felt like a new person.

But he wasn't the only one that day. A college man had been molested by a male friend of his father's and, as a result, had developed homosexual tendencies and desires. He was released. Another college man had a mother who made fun of him as he was growing up. When he was older, he started to prey upon women sexually, trying either to "get even" or finally to gain acceptance. He also prayed the prayer of release.

On another occasion, I ministered to men in a Teen Challenge rehabilitation center in Southern California. Most of them were from the streets. Some were former drug addicts, some were fresh out of prison and many had arrest records.

After we prayed the prayer of release, one young man in the front row stood up to tell the crowd that he had just forgiven his father for abandoning the family. But more difficult for him was to forgive his brother who had beaten him, molested his sisters, and insulted his mother. He said the hatred for his brother was so intense that he could use it as a tool. When he turned it loose, it released such a fury inside him that he could kill a man. I don't know if that was why he had been serving his prison sentence, but as release from that hatred boiled up and out of him, he stood there in front of everyone weeping, head bowed, never to be the same again. I stepped forward, put my arms around him, and with his head held to my shoulder, said, "I want you to feel a father's arms and know what it is to have a father's love." For him it was like a knot of bitterness inside had been untied that day, giving him the freedom to be his own man.

Those whose virginity was forcibly taken from them, who have been raped, molested, forced into incest or who were in some other way hurt by someone else — they all suffer because of someone else's sins. You see, it is not just our own sins that bother us, but through unforgiveness we actually bind the sins of others to our lives, so they bother us too. The longer we hold on to their sin through unforgiveness, the more damage it will do to our lives.

This is how sins are passed from generation to generation. Sons and daughters who do not forgive the sins of their fathers and mothers retain them and make the same mistakes with their children. Time after time in meetings when I have taught this principle, many have finally understood why they do what they do. Literally hundreds of men and women have stood and openly admitted that they are making the same mistakes with their children that their parents made with them.

But the wonderful thing is that Jesus made a way to release mistakes, errors and sins out of our lives. By receiving the power of the Holy Spirit and forgiving as God forgives, they are released from our lives, and we can live free from the mistakes of the past.

Even though many times you had no control over what was or wasn't done to you, you do have control today over how you choose to respond. Release begins with a decision by you to forgive the person who has hurt or harmed you. Picture that person and then *by faith* forgive him or her. You may not feel like forgiving, but do it by faith, taking the step of obedience by following Jesus' instructions. God doesn't say, "Can you forgive?" but rather, "Will you forgive?" As you are able to forgive them, you will find a new freedom within yourself.

After you release them, you need to reject the images and attitudes that came with them. Man communicates through word, gesture and spirit. When you accept the words and gestures of anyone, you also accept the spirit in which they were given. When you accept angry words against you, you accept the spirit of anger behind those words. When you accept lustful actions against you, you also accept the spirit of lust behind those actions.

You need to reject all that came with the sins you forgive.

Then, ask God for a fresh infilling of His Holy Spirit. Remember that Jesus said to receive the Holy Spirit and release those sins out of your life. Ask Him to search your heart and reveal to you anyone else whose sins you need to be freed from.

Pray this prayer. Mean it. Receive your release from the Lord. He said it. He will do it. Be free.

"Father, in the name of Jesus, I confess that You created me to be a man (woman) of God. You created me for a purpose and put within me everything I would need to accomplish it. I thank You for who You created me to be. I confess that all I ever want to be is that special person You created me to be.

"Now, by faith, I receive a fresh anointing of the Holy Spirit. And by the authority of Your Word in my life and the power of Your Spirit, I forgive _____ who has made my life so miserable. I forgive him (her), Lord, with all my heart.

"And now I turn toward those powers of darkness, and I say to those demon spirits: 'Get out of my life. I reject you and all your lies. I reject the image of myself that you tried to create. I am God's creation through Jesus Christ, and you have no part in my life.'

"Now, Father, I receive the righteousness and worthiness of Jesus Christ in my life. I am being changed from glory to glory, and I receive more of it right now. Thank You for it."

Now praise God to seal this work that He has done in you.

6
Receiving the Glory of Virginity

Unfortunately we live in a society in which a young man wants to get rid of his virginity at the very earliest of ages to show that he's a "man." He thinks keeping it means that he's a "wimp." A young woman wants to get rid of her virginity in order to gain acceptance. She thinks if she keeps it, she'll be considered a "prude."

Being a virgin doesn't make you an "oddball" or a "weirdo!" Being a virgin makes you the person God created you to be so that you can have a holy covenant relationship with the person He brings to you. This is His divine plan created out of love for man, in order for man and woman to become truly "one." It is something to rejoice about, not something to grumble about or for which to feel inferior! Virginity is a glory!

One young woman came running up to me after a service one night and said, "Brother Cole, this is the greatest day of my life."

"Why?" I asked.

"Because," she said, "I'm a virgin and I told someone at work who told everyone else. Now they all make fun of me. Even my own mother mocks me and asks me when I'm going to grow up, which to her means losing my virginity. I had begun to feel so guilty, so inferior and ashamed, because I was still a virgin. It's been hard for me, but tonight I've been set free from all that. Tonight I have accepted my virginity as a glory, and I thank God for it. Someday I'll be able to give it to the man I marry."

At another meeting, a sixteen-year-old man walked up to me, shook my hand and said, "Thanks."

"For what?" I asked.

He looked me right in the eye and said, "Because now I don't have to do it."

All the pressure of "proving his manhood" was gone.

Unlike these two, some have given away their virginity. There are many things other than love or physical desire that drive a person to want to give up their virginity. One young lady told me she finally realized why she had been sexually promiscuous for many years. She said that her father had always leered at the football cheerleaders on television and at other sexy-looking women, but he didn't pay any attention to her.

In order to get the attention and affection she desired, she first learned to dress sexy, and later learned to have sex with her boyfriends. She was looking for her father's love and acceptance, but since she couldn't find it, she went from boyfriend to boyfriend.

Another young lady in Dallas, Texas came to me after attending one of our meetings. Her story is tragic, but one that is repeated countless thousands of times in young girls' lives every day.

"Dr. Cole," she said, "last night in your meeting I forgave my father. I didn't have to forgive him for abusing me or for anything he did to me. I had to forgive him for what he didn't do.

"All my life as I was growing up, he never showed me any sign of affection. Because of that neglect and because I wanted so desperately to feel the affection of a man, I sought attention any way I could and became promiscuous. It almost ruined my life. Only Jesus could have saved me from a fate worse than death. But I just wanted to tell you so when you have your seminars you can tell fathers how important it is for them to show their love."

This young woman had suffered "emotional deprivation" while growing up in a normal, middle-class, Christian home. Eventually she had to forgive her father for what he hadn't done, but she also had to forgive herself for what she had done as a result.

Not only are many women hurt by emotional neglect, but many men are unable to love or be loved normally because of the lack of affection and attention in their own childhood. In Toronto, when I mentioned this fact in a meeting, I was amazed at the number of men who seemed to fall into this category. There were approximately a thousand men in attendance, and when I called for those who wanted me to let them experience for the first time a "father's hug," an avalanche of over three hundred men jammed the aisles.

Later, in Tulsa, a young professor of English at one of the major universities spoke up and told me (in front of the entire audience of men) that he had come to that meeting for the express purpose of getting a "father's hug."

Although many hurts may have happened to you along life's way, God is able to heal those hurts and help you protect the precious gift He gave to you at birth — your virginity.

Maybe you have not, for whatever reason, kept your virginity. Maybe you were neglected or didn't receive the attention you needed at a critical time in your life. Maybe you were violated by someone in some way and your virginity was taken from you. Maybe because of the hold that lust had on your mind, you gave in to temptations to have sex outside of marriage.

Maybe you are married and now realize you lost the glory of your virginity the wrong way, and you would like to have the spirit and glory of it restored to your life so you can have a covenant relationship with your husband or wife. Or maybe you are divorced or widowed and want to remarry the right way.

Know this: God cares about you, and He can bring healing and restoration into your life no matter what situation you may find yourself in today.

You may be saying to yourself right now, "My God, if only I could get my virginity back!" Even though your physical virginity may never be regained, the spirit and glory of your virginity can be restored to you. God is calling you to a life of excellence. Are you willing to identify with Him, to be someone who knows what is right and is not afraid to admit it, someone who will respond to the challenge of living a life of excellence?

I remember one meeting I held at Hofheinz Pavilion on the University of Houston campus. Almost eight thousand men were gathered there, both young and old. The final call that day was a challenge directed at the young.

Looking eyeball to eyeball with thousands of young men, I asked point-blank, "Aren't there any young men of high school or college age that have the guts or courage to do more than wallow around in the moral morass of mediocrity to which so many have sunk?

"Aren't there any young men who have guts and a love for God in their hearts, and enough of a desire to serve God that they'll 'present their bodies to God, a living sacrifice which is their reasonable service'?[1]

"Aren't there any who want the glory of God to be present in their lives through their virginity and in their decision for moral excellence?

"Aren't there any young men anywhere who want to stand up for God, admit that they want to be 'Men of God' and pay the price by developing a Godly character?

"If there is . . ."

Before I could finish my statement, hundreds of young men leaped from their chairs and began to run for the front, some jumping onto the floor of that basketball arena, to race to center court where they stood, four hundred strong, declaring their allegiance to Jesus Christ.

As they ran, the other men stood and applauded them, some of them weeping as they watched these young men who were not ashamed to be called "Men of God." It was explosive.

One young man, in the intensity of the moment, threw his bag of cocaine on the platform. Others threw things from their pockets that signified their rejection of the uncleanness in their lives.

Thank God there are young men who have that burning desire to be outstanding, men who are willing to pay the price for the true manhood which is Christ-likeness — single men who realize they need to grow and mature as men now, not wait until they are married.

You may not be a young man, and you may not have an aisle to run down or a platform to stand in front of, but right now, if you desire the spirit and glory of virginity in your life, you can ask God to give it to you today. Have integrity before God and pray this prayer with all your heart, but don't pray it unless you are serious with God.

"Father, in the name of Jesus, I'm coming to You right now because You've made me a man (woman). I want to be a man (woman) of God in every area of my life — my mind, my heart, my spirit, my body. Please forgive me for every thought, word or action that has been sinful in my life. Thank You for forgiving me.

"Thank You, Lord, that I've been born into the kingdom of God. I've been born into Your Spirit. I'm a partaker of Your Divine Nature through my Savior Jesus Christ. Satan has no rights to me. And by the authority of Your Word and the ability of Your Spirit, I rebuke the powers of darkness. I turn toward that spirit of lust, and say, 'Spirit of lust, get out of my life in the name of Jesus. I am receiving the glory of virginity, and I reject your lust.'

"And now, Lord, by faith I receive the glory of virginity into my spirit. I present to You my body — holy, acceptable, which is my reasonable service. I not only present it to You, Lord, but by the power of Your Word and Your Spirit I hold my body in the glory of virginity to present it to the woman (man) I marry as the unique gift You gave me.

"I want my sex life to be pure, holy, righteous, and good — the way You intended it to be. I don't want sin. I don't want unrighteousness. I want the glory, Lord, in my life, in my marriage — and even if I never get married. I praise You for the glory of virginity right now. Thank You, Lord."

Now praise God for it and by your thanksgiving seal the work God has done in your life. The relief and peace of God that you now feel are yours. God is working in your life. Take a moment and just be quiet in His presence. Know that He is God and that He loves you just as you are. From this day forward, you can know that He has forgiven you.

You will want to take some time daily to spend in prayer and in God's Word so that your mind will be purified and renewed. "How a man thinks" determines who he is, and from the heart "spring the issues of life."

Although quiet time with God is important, don't set unrealistic goals for your prayer life, like getting up at 4:30 in the morning to pray when you can barely get up at 6:30 now. Set time apart for God at a time you know you can give Him.

Day by day as you spend time with Him, your mind will be purified and renewed, and you will begin to notice a change taking place in your life. You will become freer in the expression of your true self, and your desires and thoughts will begin to change. As you begin to think differently, your decisions will change, and you will notice a difference in your lifestyle. Some changes

will happen right away while other changes
will come only over a period of time. Be
patient with yourself and know that God is
at work within you as long as you continue
to yield yourself to Him to continue working
His purpose in your life.

7

Resisting Peer Pressure

You have just received the spirit of virginity which is a part of the cleansing of unrighteousness. Your sexuality has been translated into the Kingdom of God, and He is giving you a new beginning in this area of your life. Be aware, however, that there are other areas of your life that have not yet been renewed and that temptations will continue to come. You will need to remain firm in the commitment you have made. God will be with you.

Loneliness, fear, fatalism, hopelessness and cynicism run rampant in high schools and colleges today. You may have felt this way before. But loneliness and being alone are two entirely different things.

Being alone is sometimes necessary, healthy, desirable and appreciated. Loneliness never is. That's the reason for so many singles clubs, friendship centers and dating services. Friends are the antidote to loneliness.

Finding acceptance always seems to require initiation. People are initiated into clubs, fraternities, smoking and sex. The initiation can be painful, humiliating, exhilarating, exciting or depressing, depending upon the rejection or acceptance.

The ministry of the Lord Jesus Christ to the human heart is to heal completely the trauma of loneliness and any form of rejection. When you are ministered to by the Lord with His healing, His acceptance, His power and His grace for your life, it gives you the ability to face the world and its reality. It gives you a security the world cannot match nor understand.

Jesus gives a peace, an inner stability, that is a mystery to the world but a comfort to the believer. You can trust God's Spirit in you to bring that peace from the nature of Christ into your life as needed. But you must be yielded to the Spirit in every area of your life to experience peace. Holding on to any sin will create confusion that will keep you from experiencing peace.

When you allow yourself to be intimidated into doing what your mind and heart know is wrong, you weaken your resolve to do right and impair your decision-making ability.

Whatever you give into in life grows stronger, while what you resist grows weaker. In order to know what to resist and what to yield to, you must know what is right. Joseph knew that fornication and adultery were not "right," so when Potiphar's wife tried to seduce him, he fled. A foolish man would have said, "I can stay here and not give in." Running away is sometimes the best response to evil.

Eventually, a person who entertains evil temptation begins to waver between right and wrong because he doesn't make a decision. A man like this professes to hate sin but still has a lingering love for it. As a result, he will continue to be tempted to yield to evil. Over a period of time, his ability to distinguish between right and wrong will become weaker and weaker. The lusts of his flesh will begin to overtake him, and he will end up saying yes instead of no.

Many are the young men and women who said *yes* to friends when they were invited to "fool around" instead of doing what they knew was right. Saying *no* to a friend *then* would have enabled them to say *yes* to their talent and intelligence later. It takes courage to resist the peer pressure of your friends — firmness not to go with the crowd.

When our Lord Jesus Christ faced temptation, He overcame it through quoting the Word of God to the devil. He didn't just say *no*, but was able to give the reason for saying it. The devil departed and left Jesus alone. Then the Bible says Jesus "returned in the power of the Spirit."

His submission to the Father, resistance to the devil, and refusal to sin, strengthened His spirit and added stature to His manhood. In addition, He had memorized vast portions of Scripture that gave weight to His words. The principle applies to all of life: *Success is based on the ability to say no.*

Rob is a young man I've known off and on for a number of years. When he makes a commitment to the Lord, he comes around to see me. When it wears off, he stays away.

When he was in high school, Rob had a close relationship with the Lord and showed a tremendous capacity for leadership. But after being rejected by his mother because of his Christian faith and being rejected by a Christian girlfriend because he did not control his youthful lusts, he believed he had to prove himself to women and became double-minded.

He says he loves the Lord in his heart, yet he wallows in promiscuity, lewd behavior and addictions. He is unproductive in his work, can't find a steady girlfriend and swings constantly from one extreme to another. He is unstable in all his ways.

To top it off, he excuses his failures because of what happened with his mother and girlfriend in high school. Rob will never be a success until he decides who he is going to serve — God or himself.

Because of an intense desire to belong and be accepted among his peers, he gave in to "peer pressure" or the "fear of man." At its root is the fear of rejection and the driving need to receive approval from others, especially peers.

The truth is, the less we fear man, the more respect we gain. Just take a look at successful men in this world. Without exception, they overcame their fear of man. When they did, they became bold in their confession and bold in their identification with their belief, product or activity. In short, they became overcomers.

People who overcome the fear of man are spiritual achievers. Billy Graham is just one example of a man who has overcome. What do you think of when you hear his name? Christianity and a lot more.

While still in his teens, Billy walked down an aisle after an evangelistic meeting with Mordecai Ham and made a total commitment to the Lord. In his early twenties he was preaching outdoors when William Randolph Hearst wrote a cryptic note to his newspaper editors in Los Angeles. It said, "Puff Graham."

Daily, Billy Graham was in the headlines. Soon, everywhere he went, people recognized him as the young man who was preaching about Jesus Christ. Anything he had been prior to that time was gone, and he became totally identified with Jesus Christ.

Since then, his name has become a household word in homes around the world — and everywhere people associate him with Jesus Christ. He lost his life in identification with Jesus Christ, then he found a life he never would have known otherwise.

It is the same way with you. You find life by losing it. The choice is yours. The glory is God's.

Act with courage in the classroom, on the campus, at home and on the job. Don't wait until your youth is gone to get the guts or the wisdom to make your life count for God. Do it now! That one decision can make you a success.

Jim, the student body president of a high school, appeared on the *700 Club* television program recently to tell how things in school had become so bad that he decided to do something about it. He ran for student body president, then gathered others around him who were all-out for God. Together they changed his school. Rather than being intimidated by others, he made the decision to be an influence on them.

Everything Jim dreamed could happen on his campus, he prayed for and worked toward. As he stood fast, he saw his dreams become reality. He is nationally known today as a single high school student who made a difference.

Steve was a young man whose good looks opened doors that other guys only dreamed of. Although he and his roommate both had church backgrounds, they led a bar-hopping, promiscuous lifestyle. One day their guilt was bothering them so much, his roommate suggested they turn their lives back to God. It seemed like a good idea, so they knelt together at the couch in their house and prayed a simple prayer. His roommate quickly went back to his old lifestyle, but Steve determined he would be as committed to his new life as he had been to his old. As Steve applied himself to the Word, God showed him how he could go into business for himself. He started the company he now runs and although he is still young, today he serves as the men's director at a large church.

Chuck was a drug-dealing, surf-riding, hippie-looking beach bum when he first heard about Jesus Christ. His only positive quality was a natural head for business, and salvation sounded like a good deal. "You mean, all my sins will be totally wiped away, and I get to spend eternity in heaven?" he asked his minister. "And all I have to do is give God my life? Life isn't doing me much good anyway, so I'll sign up!"

It was such a good deal, Chuck couldn't help but tell other people about it. Within weeks he had prayed with several people for salvation. Today Chuck has an international business and, although he is not a professional minister, he has won thousands of people to Christ.

Jamal was the vice-president of a motorcycle club. "I wasn't just toying with the enemy," he says, "I was on staff." He heard about Jesus Christ and knew he had found the love he had always wanted. When he realized he ought to give back everything he had ever stolen, the only thing he legally owned was the jean jacket his brother had given him. He returned everything and even reported himself to the police. He rides the mountains now, ministering to men who are running from the law and are lost to society.

You may not be Billy Graham, or a Steve or Chuck or Jamal, but you have the same ability within you to overcome the fear of man. You may be ridiculed, mocked or rejected, but it is never too late to say "no": "no" to illicit sex, "no" to a wrong engagement, "no" to sin. Saying "no" on the day of the wedding is difficult, but it is far easier than a disastrous marriage. Saying "no" after you have led someone to believe you want to engage in sex won't make you popular on earth, but it will make you popular in heaven. It is never too late to say "no." Don't say "yes" to sin just because someone intimidates you. Honor God more than man.

And if you do sin, repent. No sin is too great for God's forgiveness. Yours is no exception. God's grace is great for all. The natural results of sin are guilt, fear and hiding. Don't feel too guilty or be too afraid to go to God. Don't try to hide from Him. Go to God immediately.

Satan can only spoil your life through temptation or accusation. Even if you don't succumb to the temptation, he will accuse you as if you did. Reject it. Only repent for what you have really done, not for what Satan tries to accuse you of doing. Let the Holy Spirit be your guide, not "the fiery darts of the wicked."[1]

If you find that you absolutely cannot date without sinning, then don't date. Instead, allow God to be your friend, confidant, counselor, the One Who knows you best, accepts you just as you are and loves you perfectly. Let Him be the One to

Whom you can go at any time, under any conditions. Become His friend and grow into an ever-increasing friendship with Him. Don't waste your youth. Don't give up your life because of loneliness. God is right there with you. Allow Him to fulfill your desires by bringing to you human companionship and a spouse.

If you do decide to get married, don't get married just to have a "steady date" or "legal sex," and don't get divorced thinking it will rid you of your problems. Marrying the wrong person or quitting a marriage will only make life more difficult, not easier. Remember, success is based on the ability to say "no," not the ability to say "yes."

If you are not yet married, thrust your life into the Kingdom of God now as the Holy Spirit directs. It will not make you "too spiritual" to find a spouse, but it will save you a lot of painful growing later on.

Whether married or single, find peace and security in a friendship with God and allow Him to work out the details of your life.

God's purpose for you is to go from glory to glory and to enjoy the true glory of your wedding by entering marriage ready for the glory of sex.

What is your decision?

If you have never received Jesus Christ as your personal Lord and Savior, why not do it right now? Simply repeat this prayer with sincerity: "Lord Jesus, I believe that You are the Son of God. I believe that You became man and died on the cross for my sins. I believe that God raised You from the dead and made You the Savior of the world. I confess that I am a sinner and I ask You to forgive me, and to cleanse me of all my sins. I accept Your forgiveness, and I receive You as my Lord and Savior. In Jesus' name, I pray. Amen."

"...if you confess with your mouth, 'Jesus is Lord,' and believe in your heart that God raised him from the dead, you will be saved. For it is with your heart that you believe and are justified, and it is with your mouth that you confess and are saved....for, 'Everyone who calls on the name of the Lord will be saved.'"

Romans 10:9,10,13 NIV

"If we confess our sins, he is faithful and just and will forgive us our sins and purify us from all unrighteousness."

1 John 1:9 NIV

Now that you have accepted Jesus as your Savior:

1. Read your Bible *daily*. It is spiritual food that will make you a strong Christian.

2. Pray and talk to God daily. He desires for the two of you to communicate and share your lives with each other.

3. Share your faith with others. Be bold to let others know that Jesus loves them.

4. Regularly attend a local church where Jesus is preached, where you can serve Him and where you can fellowship with other believers.

5. Let His love in your heart touch the lives of others by your good works done in His name.

Please let us know of the decision you made. Write:

Honor Books
P.O. Box 55388
Tulsa, OK 74155

References

Chapter 1
[1]Genesis 1:26
[2]Ephesians 5:31

Chapter 2
[1]Romans 4:3
[2]Genesis 17:5
[3]Hebrews 9:22 TLB
[4]Romans 12:1

Chapter 3
[1]Deuteronomy 22:15
[2]Deuteronomy 22:19
[3]Deuteronomy 22:20,21
[4]Proverbs 1:7
[5]Ephesians 5:25

Chapter 4
[1]James 4:17

Chapter 5
[1]John 20:22,23 AMP

Chapter 6
[1]Romans 12:1

Chapter 7
[1]Ephesians 6:16

Edwin Louis Cole, founder and president of the Christian Men's Network, speaks with a prophetic voice to the men of this generation. His message that "Manhood and Christlikeness are synonymous"  declares a standard for manhood that has changed hundreds of thousands of lives. He is an internationally acclaimed speaker, television personality, bestselling author and motivational lecturer. Cole travels extensively, showing men how to realize their dream of real manhood by looking to Jesus Christ as their role model.

Books by Edwin Louis Cole

Facing the Challenge of Crisis and Change

Courage: A Book for Champions

Maximized Manhood

The Potential Principle

Communication, Sex and Money

Invest to Increase

Entering and Leaving Crisis and Change

The Unique Woman

For a list of cassette tapes or videos
by Edwin Louis Cole
or for a free copy of the "Manhood Today"
newspaper, write:

Edwin Louis Cole Ministries
The Christian Men's Network
P. O. Box 610588
Dallas, Texas 75261

Tulsa, Oklahoma 74155